Abyss

YA HSIEN

TRANSLATED BY

John Balcom

ZEPHYR PRESS

BROOKLINE, MA

Zephyr Press, a non-profit arts and education 501(c)(3) organization,
publishes literary titles that foster a deeper understanding of cultures
and languages. Zephyr Press books are distributed to the trade in the U.S.
and Canada by Consortium Book Sales and Distribution [www.cbsd.com]
and by Small Press Distribution [www.spdbooks.org].

Zephyr Press acknowledges with gratitude the financial support of the
Massachusetts Cultural Council and of Mr. Tzu-hsien Tung, Chairman of the
Pegatron Corporation, who assisted in the publication of this book.

massculturalcouncil.org

Cataloguing-in publication data is available from the Library of Congress.

ISBN 978-1-938890-21-5

ZEPHYR PRESS
50 Kenwood Street
Brookline, MA 02446

www.zephyrpress.org

Contents

Songs Without Music
—BOOK 3

Collection of Broken Columns
—BOOK 4

Profiles
—BOOK 5

Weeds
—BOOK 6

Setting Out from Sensations
—BOOK 7

Abyss

Anatomy

—prefatory poem

There was a man
Who truly was as gaunt as Jesus.
He longed to be crucified,
(and hence perhaps gain fame)
To wear a blood-spattered robe,
To have a crown of thorns
   —even if only made of paper—
Placed upon his rudely mocked
And despised forehead.
   But, alas, the price of white poplar rose!
Nails went into building skyscrapers,
People nearly all lost interest
In being Philistines
Or a man like Saint Simon
To have curses spit upon his not so prominent nose,
To take his place beneath
A second cross.
   There was a man
Who thought such things after the sun set.

Wild Water Chestnuts

—BOOK I

Spring Days

Oh God, the *suona* have sounded
Winter is like an amputee's sleeve
Empty, dark, and tediously long

Oh God
Permit us to see the shadow of your robe
On the face of the sundial
On blades of grass, on the first heads of clover
Seek and find
Your bloody footprints

We hope to hear your new song
From the twelve holes of a willow flute
From the talk of wind and sea

Oh God, the *suona* have sounded
Commanding those white spirits
(Who, all winter long, knit woolen caps for the mountain peaks)
To return by stream and rivulet
To the lakes and marshes, their old homes

Give the boys a grassy slope to roll their iron hoops
Give the girls dry ground to spin their tops
Oh God, direct the sun
To set upon the dragon-headed cane
Of that old woman basking in the sun

Oh God
Scatter fresh blossoms on the road traveled by the sedan chairs
Moisten their lips with rose water
Permit them a kiss

Where there is no crossing build no ferry
Let them feel the cold, the warmth of your currents
And with rose, hairy caltrop, and jujube tree
Prod them, make them feel a gentle pain

The *suona* have sounded, Oh God!
Fill our vocal cords with your voice
When we part
The tassels of the bridal palanquin
And discover spring days seated within

Autumn Song

—for Nuan-nuan, my Warmth

The fallen leaves are the final spasm
Reed flowers vanish in the pond's blue eye
Sounds from the washing stones in July grow faint
Nuan-nuan, my Warmth

Geese no longer write beautiful sonnets
In the high autumn sky
Nuan-nuan, my Warmth

Horses leave broken blossoms under hoof
On a narrow mountain path in the South
A singer leaves a broken note
In a dark temple in the North

Autumn, nothing remains of autumn
Except a little warmth

Like a little warmth
Everything remains

A Woman

Behind that woman
Swing the streets of Florence
Like a portrait, she approaches

If I kiss her
Raphael's oils will stick
To this foreign mustache of mine

Ringdove

Girls are rolling brass hoops
Far away the ringdove sings

Far away the ringdove sings
High in the birch tree sits my dream

Far away the ringdove sings
Nerval's lobster blocks my way
For a blond maiden's blue girdle
Ill-tempered Byron and I duel

Far away the ringdove sings
D'Annunzio sniffs a withered rose
A ship sails to where Sappho plunged into the sea
And I'm a galley slave with a lash-scarred back

Far away the ringdove sings
My dream falls from the birch tree

The sun too is rolling a brass hoop
Far away the ringdove sings

Wild Water Chestnuts

I saw her off to southern shores
And then I wept
The wild water chestnuts wept too

I don't know if Mallarme cried
On the seventh page of a thick book
   I ran into him last autumn
He was silent
The wild water chestnuts were silent too

Cocteau's spirit
Dwelt in a profusion of shells
I put dozens of them in her straw hat
In a whisper I asked if she liked the shells' whorls
And in a whisper asked the water chestnuts too

Petofi went far away to wage revolution
They like to shed blood
We like to shed tears
   The wild water chestnuts like to shed tears too

And so, on southern shores
The wild water chestnuts blossomed
Crying till Vega rose in the sky

Melancholia

Bracken sprouts in the monastery
Like nuns, in spring
It's as if they were not melancholy
But they are

I once
Discovered melancholy
Braided with coarse hemp rope
In the red beard of a Portuguese sailor
Dancing madly on top of a table

A popular songstress sang:
I was so happy I could die
She laughed gaily, melancholy
Hidden in the strings of a mandolin
Though she laughed gaily

At dusk housewives close their doors
Melancholy, holding goat tails in its mouth
Enters the palisade
And seals the baby's eyes

Between two pairs of kissing lips
Melancholy is held
Like a flower bud
Holding
The whole spring

Yes, it's especially in spring when
I think of some bracken, some sailors
Some mandolins
A few closed doors
A little melancholy

Only melancholy has no melancholy
Yes, especially in spring
Only that lacking in melancholy
Is melancholic

Song

Who is crying in the distance?
Why is it so sad?
Ride a golden horse and see
That it's the past

Who is crying in the distance?
Why is it so sad?
Ride a gray horse and see
That it's the future

Who is crying in the distance?
Why is it so sad?
Ride a white horse and see
That it's Love

Who is crying in the distance?
Why is it so sad?
Ride a black horse and see
That it's Death

1980

The aged sun drips down through the castor bean plants,
That'll be 1980.

We'll have a small wooden house
Built one spring,
And it'll have a red roof like in a fairy tale
And grassy slopes all around with cattle grazing
And it'll be in Australia.

The clover, in a hubbub of color
Will dispel all loneliness.

Clouds will
Drift from the mountain hollows at dawn
Drift back at dusk
With nothing else to do.

The sky will have so much blue
You'll ask if we can borrow some to dye Shan-shan's skirt
   (How do I know!)

We'll place a small cistern of water behind the house.
The Dog Star will often steal a drink there,
Orion will also often steal a drink there
And round-faced children, too, will steal a drink there.

The cows will be docile;
The day before the wheat-harvest festival
They'll silently give us badly needed milk!
Milk with a hint of green, green grass,
Shan-shan doesn't like the grassy taste.

The valleys are far away
With nothing to send us
Send us some songs, some echoes.
You said
That's good enough.

When winter comes, snow will cover the windows
We'll kindle the fallen leaves gathered in autumn,
Mao-mao gathered the most,
Mao-mao is a good boy,
Mao-mao gathered the most.

I say I want to go to the small town
To buy some Christmas cards
The stockings ought to be hung on the mantel,
The Southern Cross should also revolve to Jerusalem.

You ask what's so pretty about the cards
Don't we live in a card?
By way of argument, I say
We don't need to put anything between slices of bread
We can just put our smiles there.

We argue until you call for a song!
Singing is always good.
The children are all asleep,
The candlewick has budded many times.

I ask why you are still making clothes.
What will you have to do all those tomorrows?

The following day the aged sun again drips through the castor bean plants,
That'll be 1980.

Funeral Parlor

Vultures rise from behind the funeral parlor
Our necks are bedecked in fresh flowers
(Why has Mother still not come?)

The men trim their beards one last time
The women touch-up their lipstick one last time
Deciding never again to attend another dance

Holding a cane that'll never tap the ground again
Light and shadow
   Will never play again on glasses astride a nose
And the girl's purple handkerchiefs will
   Never again hold sweet strawberries on a spring outing
(Why has Mother still not come?)

And that copy of *Simon* under the pillow
I'm too lazy to read it a second time
Life's secret
Was originally stored in this long, black-lacquered, wooden box

Is tomorrow spring?
Sitting in a palanquin
We wonder what there is to see at the crossroads

Is it someone's birthday tomorrow?
Dressed in such fine satin clothes
Excitedly, we row to the bridge by Grandma's house

And the vultures rise from behind the church
For what do the priest's organ pipes sob?
What is it the nuns mumble?
(Why has Mother still not come?)

She said that come next Tomb Sweeping Festival
She'd plant a small white poplar for me
I don't like that rustling sound
It's so mournful, isn't it?

Ah, what wriggles behind the pupils?
What festivities bring the maggots together?
And why are there no tears to drink?
(Why has Mother still not come?)

The Snake's Clothes

My wife is a woman
Who thinks her dowry allows her a nasty temper.
Her blue belt was washed and washed
Washed and washed. And later hung out to dry
On the dahlias.
Later (persistently)
    She sings
      A ditty.

My wife wishes
To wear
Every earthly blossom,
Leaving not a single bud for the neighbor girls!
On her *qipao*, she stitches and sews
Stitches and sews a crying peacock. My wife always
Believes dressmaking is more important than Congress.

Even though we share the same sun
    (So my wife thinks)
With America,
The husbands there are lazy too
    (I was in the middle of buying jam)
But I wasn't singing
    Singing
      A ditty.

In spring
My wife
Resembles an egret clinging to
Her small pool—a mirror.
In spring, my wife thinks and thinks
Thinks and thinks
Decides to borrow clothes from a rat snake

Under the Barber Pole

The barbers sing

It's always the same wheat-harvest festival
It's always an abundance of rye without ears
It's always reaped, reaped
On the land of inspiration
A small southern path leads to ears of grain
And it's also a kind of horticultural school
A kind of beauty
A kind of agricultural reform
A kind of taste for something other than Greek sculpture

The barbers sing

Dawn

—on the balcony

At dawn
When the earth shows a patch of American sky
To a Chinese chrysanthemum
I remember
    Yesterday, the name I used yesterday

Passing through the corridor's brown
There are girls in the guava tree
Drying their moist,
    vegetal souls
And the phonograph of the neighbor's mill turns
    (Offenbach rides a donkey)
And begins to grind the aged millet

I remember
The name I used
The day before the day before yesterday
Sitting on the balcony in silk pajamas facing the sea
I folded the love you gave me like an autumn fan
I try to return
    To a classicism
    Of the flower embossed handle of a silver spoon sort

But it's dawn
When the earth shows a Chinese chrysanthemum
To a patch of American sky
Reading a newspaper from the provincial capital
I suddenly realize how long it's been
    Since God last paid a visit

Wartime

—BOOK 2

Temple of the Earth God

Far, far away
On a narrow and desolate shore
The North Star draws water with its dipper

Offers night
Black wine

Night
Sends it on bat wings
As a gift for the Earth God

In a small incense burner
In shallow earthen vessels
The wine clamors
Waiting for someone to take a drink

But the bumblebees just grumble
(Their homes are too cramped)
In the Earth God's ears

Squirrels like nothing better that to eat on the sly
The candles from years gone by

In the grass the field cricket intones
He is a poet
But with no taste for wine

The wine grows boisterous

The Earth God silently smiles a wry smile
(He's smiled wryly for hundreds of years)
Since those days
Wine has not wet his whiskers

Since the Earth God's old lady
Died in the wind
Died in the rain
Died under the naughty scythes of reaping lads

Mountain God

Hunting horns shake last year's pinecones to the ground
The cliff road chants softly with the hoof beats of a pilgrim's donkey
While melting snow resembles silver thread spun by a spinster
A shepherd boy sharpens his sickle on a stone Buddha's toe
Spring, ah, spring
I feed a wanderer's horse under a bodhi tree

In rocky strata, veins of ore gasp
The sun kindles a fire in the forest
As a sick, old woman tries to peddle her sour apples at a down shop
Life drips from a weasel's red eyes
Summer, ah, summer
I bang the rusty knocker on a sick man's door

Rustic melodies frolic in baskets on the backs of village girls
Weeping geese cry for the clouds to wait
As the feeble old sun parts his beard to lick persimmons in the wood
The red leaves large enough to hold quatrains
Autumn, ah, autumn
I help a fisherman work his nets in a small stream in misty rain

The woodcutter's axe sings in a deep valley
A cold-fearing tomcat rests in an old woman's arms
As the north wind whistles in the chimney
People in reed-lined boots spin tops on a frozen pond
Winter, ah, winter
I warm myself with a beggar by a fire under the cracked bell
    of an ancient temple

War God

At night
A night of many black crosses
An ailing clock tower, two dead sisters: hour and minute hands
The frozen arms draw the final V

V? There is only Death, black victory
This is a year of famine. Many mothers bewail
The deaths of their children, a little fifteen-year-old white poplar
Yesterday's skirt is no longer worn

Wineskin broken, a thrusting Damascus sword
The bugles are silent, so are the torches
Someone lies on a broken shield
Women moan, babies are wrapped in torn flags

Many fields are trampled, buckwheat flowers wither
At Waterloo, paste on a few bloody eyeballs
Brass spurs, a general's defeat
The War God shines his boots

Many black crosses have no names
The vultures' cold feast, the dreary gorging
The ailing clock tower, two dead sisters
Their frozen arms drawing the final V

Beggar

Don't know what'll happen after spring comes
What'll happen to the snow
What'll happen to the robins and puppies
    After spring comes

The same Kuan Ti Temple
The same laundered socks drying on the crescent moon
The same tune and lotus flowers falling as before
Jujube tree, jujube tree
Everyone's sun is shining, shining
    On the jujube tree

What matters is
I don't have a cent
To give to my memories, squashed like dead lice
To give to my grass sandals, worn out on the road
To give to my desire for slaughter
    Hidden in the battlements of my teeth

Every door is closed to me, when night falls
People begin to cherish the walls they've built round themselves
Only the moonlight, only the moonlight has no walls
And will fill my broken alms bowl with the milk of charity
    When night, when night falls

Who strikes his own profile on the gold coins
    (Hey-ho, the lotus flowers fall as before)
Who throws his rank in the dust
    (Hey-ho, the ditty is sung as before)

Jujube tree, jujube tree
Everyone's sun is shining, shining
    On the jujube tree

Spring, who knows what'll happen after spring comes
Snow, robins, puppies
And will my walking stick blossom?
    And after blossoming, what then?

Capital City

Ah, Capital City
Hurry and chew those ancient memories
With your last toothed battlements
The eternal flame is about to die out
    at the end of the winding corridor
Not a single Tartar's horse is seen across the vast desert
By the light of the moon

That age is long gone
    On a shield, in a tiger tent
That age is long gone
    Under a dragon banner, in armor

The ruts of the compass cart went the way of oracle bones
    Lost and forgotten
Ah, Capital City, today your wheels roll
On cold, cold rails of iron
A metallic order, a steely life
A new form of entertainment
Opened at the factory
Ah! Amplitude! Speed! Violence!
Steel songs, iron words, metallic cries of the city
    Love of wheel and rut
    Marriage of nut and bolt
New heat rash, new convulsions
Ah, Capital City, your pure grass plumes
Can no longer praise
The girls' faces twisted in a frenzied dance
At dusk, at seven o'clock

The heart of an entire nation begins to drip
Drip blood, begins to suffer from radiation sickness
Till a rat-gray fear
Of nuclear fission
Lies beneath the underground cables
And on plates of pudding and sandwiches

Ah, Capital City
Hurry and chew those fading memories
With your last toothed battlements
Your drum tower no longer beats out the modern age
The eternal flame dies out, dies out
In the setting sun

Red Corn

The wind blew during the reign of the last emperor
Blew over that string of red corn

Hanging there
Under the eaves
As if the entire northland
The melancholy of the entire northland
Were hanging there

Like afternoons spent playing hooky
The snow froze the private teacher's ruler
My cousin's mule was tethered beneath the mulberry tree

Like when the *suona* began to sound
The Taoist priests mumbled
Grandpa's soul departed for the capital
    but had not returned

Like brother's calabash tucked in a padded gown
A little dreary, a little warm
And brass hoops rolled over the hills
Upon seeing grandma's buckwheat field in the distance
We broke into tears

Only that kind of corn is red
Hung for ages there
Under the eaves
The wind blew during the reign of the last emperor

You'll never understand
The sight of red corn
Hanging there under the eaves
And it's color
Neither does my daughter born in the South
Nor Verhaeren

And now that
I have grown old
Red corn hangs
Under the eaves of memory
The wind of 1958 blows
The red corn hangs there

Salt

Granny never met Dostoyevsky. In spring she said only one thing: Salt, salt, give me a handful of salt! The angels sang in the elm trees. That year, the peas hardly blossomed at all.

The Minister of Salt and his camel caravan journeyed along the coast, seven hundred miles away. Granny's blind eyes had never seen seaweed. She only repeated one thing: Salt, salt, give me a handful of salt! The angels laughed and sprinkled her with snow.

In 1911, the Party members reached Wuchang. Hanging the bands of cloth for binding her feet in the elms, Granny went off in the breath of wild dogs and on the wings of vultures. And many were the mournful voices on the wind crying: Salt, salt, give me a handful of salt! That year the peas were covered with white blossoms. And Dostoyevsky never met Granny.

Wartime

—Loyang, 1942

After spring
Incendiary bombs lift the streets like a fan
On a splintered
Sandalwood chair
My mother's hard smile
   rises as a memory of sorts

Slender-legged bees built their hive in Seven-li Temple
My mother was half concealed amid last year's
Many dove-gray deaths
And when the world did the same thing
Her shoulders were made of stone

That night, between regret and drowsiness
A donkey brayed all night long and a file of soldiers
Walked beneath my window posting proclamations
On the telephone poles
The lush rhododendrons bent down
And it's said no one slept

But from start to finish
Their intention was to make you choose a river
To reluctantly find an end
Or to write a long epistle to your skinny, little woman
   in another county
Or to frighten a field of buckwheat

But it's already been done
People are weary of keeping watch. And no matter what
You must sooner or later take part in the making of grass
In the hum of Death
Even the angels are not needed

Songs Without Music

—BOOK 3

Sensations of the High Seas

The mutinous sea raises a white flag
The vast horizon stands upright, upside down
In wind and rain the gulls cry forlornly
Sweeping past the blind eyes of the ship's figurehead
(Their wings, moist and salty)

Vertigo rests on the dishes in the galley
In the jackfruit and the sturgeon
In the faded lipstick of female tourists

Time
A pendulum. A swing
A rocking horse. A cradle
Time

Brain reeling, topsy-turvy
Stirring the remaining memories of when
    two feet last touched land
Leftover memories, the topsy-turvy flow of lingering memories

Through the porthole the sea line lists
And it's time again for coffee

Voyage of Death

Night. A reef
Death's thirteen-day voyage

The signal lights give ill-omened curses
The bells echo

The atrophied souls of the passengers
Meager and mossy
Frightfully parasitize
An old navigation chart, a plummet
And the captain's compass

The bells echo

The mast shudders
The rusty weathercock
Pecks at the crumbs of the stars

And as the evening prayers of the seasick spin
The eyes of twin Kings on the bridge table are silent
Perhaps a sedative would be slightly more effective than Jesus

Shipboard Rats

Seeing the lights on the west coast of Luzon
I think of my gray brothers living there
Happily exercising their jaws

There are so many bakeries in Manila
That was 1954
There was a black girl
Who'd give a kiss for half a walnut
Now she lives in the ship's cabin
Takes her kids
To dream, pillowed on the ocean's flow
She doesn't like needlework

The Chinese captain wasn't in favor of the marriage
Though I promised to eat no more holes in his uniform pockets
Nor in his logbooks with red spines

My wife says it was smart to run wild
Perhaps we've been able to put the fear of cats behind us

I say there are worse things
There are reefs out there
We know about
But the captain does not

Of course it's pointless to fret over tomorrow's windsock
So long as we can exercise our jaws with something today

A Song Without Music

Coo for love like the doves
Sport any flower on your lapel
Dance those irrational but joyful dances
Embrace with the same gravitational pull as the earth
Spin! Let your skirt shake up all aesthetics
Ah, I fear the sadness to come on the heels of May
   (Oh, Nana, don't talk to me of Zola)
It's too simple for friends to compare life to pomegranates
I don't want to know why we must go to sea
You want to paint green and gold nudes
He wants to write poems throughout the starry night
Anyway, I fear the sadness to come on the heels of May
Ah, so hold her waist held by so many others!
   (Oh, Simon, go trample de Gourmont's fallen leaves)
Mount Heaven with the moon
Delve hell with a spring
Marry on a whim
Dream different dreams under one roof
Kiss those silly lips, but not those sillier lips
   (O, Loti, does the Dadaist pistol really shoot music?)
Ah, wind, fire, sea, and land
War, laurels, all kinds of fascinating revolutions
Write blazing words with blood on abandoned palace walls
Your childhood returned in full to God

Sailors, a Romance

Here on land we stand, here on land
In French shoes we vigorously trample spring underfoot

The vegetables from Honolulu have all wilted
Trade winds in the Bashi Channel change direction
Tonight we may love
And even old Jesus will have nothing to say about it
Our salty beards
Our chests tattooed with green dragons
Tonight we may love
And even old Jesus will have nothing to say about it

The captain stole and sold so many of our springs

Flood the city streets with beer
With the string of a strange whistle
Bind the wings of small, timid doves
In a few filthy alleyways
    —it's just a philosophy

Set fire to bolts of cloth
Send the carpenters, smiths, and painters packing
    (And everything for building ships)
And find a pair of scarlet-painted fingernails
To murder the captain's seafaring heart
    —it's just a philosophy

The captain stole and sold many of our springs

Quickly gulp down love
Like a bull
For just as on past nights we lost land
We'll mull over love
Like a bull chewing its cud

This plant called woman
Planted on deck, she won't grow
But here on land, she'll grow, here on land
This plant called woman

The captain stole and sold so many of our springs

In French shoes we vigorously trample spring underfoot
We stand, here on land we stand
Afternoon in a Bar

Here we kill
Kill a whole afternoon's pallor
I trample the Persian garden on the tiles
My friend spits pieces of chestnut shells
On the face of some anonymous princess

Chinese pagodas are embroidered on the curtains
Several court officials cross a jade bridge
Discussing the Qing dynasty or the Tang
Their audience tablets always hide
Another side of their souls

Suddenly it seems
We allow a little spring in
Though girls are not tantamount to spring
Nor are paper flowers or what's left of last night's make-up

If you test those falsies with your fingertips
Or search a pile of golden teeth with your tongue

And we gulp down chrysanthemum tea
(It doesn't matter who picked it)
Madly inhale the dizziness of cheap tobacco

Crack dirty jokes about girls from nice families
And kill all the pallor of this afternoon
And a little of tomorrow afternoon's
Yes, tomorrow afternoon
Our shoes will surely get us that far

A Night in Kuling Forest

Little Mother, burn this fennel
Little Mother, give me your blood

And let me be you for one night
When the dewdrops cry hoarsely from the window
Jesus will no longer see us
I'll cover you, cover your naked body
With my hair
Clothed thus, you'll suffer no more

And be jealous too
And mumble as well
    —about some sort of herb
As the evening star appears
Clamoring herbs
Multiply beneath the streetlights
    Blocking pedestrians
That feeling of danger
No one would face even with a scythe
That feeling of danger

And so
Between twin cliffs like pillows
Like two sea beasts cooled in air
Allowing souls to twist, to twine,
To adhere together on their tongues
Poisoning one another to death
            (Wait till daybreak, then we won't hear the noise on the
                landlady's stairway . . .)

Afterwards, we'll set off, following the river
Cover my earrings with a baseball cap
Take me to see the tides and the flowers
As if I were your little brother
Afterwards, we'll set off again, following the river
Cross the night, these stars
The black beauty
Cross these bed sheets
Bed sheets were originally our kingdom

Little Mother, I give you my name
Little Mother, give me yours

Collection of Broken Columns

—BOOK 4

On the Streets of China

Dreams and the blotting paper of moonlight
Poets wear corduroy suits
Nu Wa can't be reached by public telephone
Thought goes the way of oracle bone script
So join the muse in some wheat gruel from a bronze vessel
Sandwiches and beefsteaks slowly grow lonely
Poets wear corduroy suits

The Yellow Emperor shouts from the dust
With trackless trolleys, our imperial carriages rust away
Since there are now gas lamps and neon lights
We no longer need to loan them our old sun
Just remember that battle with Zhi Yu
Just remember Leizu's lovely silk-spinning song
Just remember when poets did not wear corduroy suits

There is no parliament nothing happened either
Confucius never considered taxing Laozi's royalties
Planes roar over a row of smoldering willows
The student movement strikes against the palace walls
There's no coffee; incredibly, Li Bai could write poetry
    and never make a revolution
Much less corduroy suits

Whitman's volumes of poetry didn't come out of Dunhuang
The ocean liners tell that beyond the four seas lie four more
Beggars in subways hold out black bowls
Sailors flirt with scantily clad women

To the left: red lights; to the right, red lights
And poets wear corduroy suits

A quinine ad is pasted on Shen Nong's face
As soon as spring arrives, everyone is debating interplanetary travel
Steam whistles strangle workers, pamphlets on democracy, bus stops,
   lawyers and electric chairs
Heads are no longer publicly displayed above city gates
Fuxi's eight trigrams will never be awarded the Nobel Prize
The Qufu cypresses have been made into railroad ties
If you wear anything, wear a corduroy suit

Dreams and the blotting paper of moonlight
Poets wear corduroy suits
Everyone says there is no such thing as a dragon
So join the muse in some wheat gruel from a bronze vessel
So thought goes the way of oracle bone script
Just wait for this sexy flick to end
Just wear corduroy suits

Babylon

Wash the princess' hair with plantain juice
Bind the parrot to its perch with a chain of braided silver
Place a golden cockerel on the cold tiles of the palace
Cover the marble portico with a white leopard skin
    I am a black slave girl

The hammering of horse's hooves wakes the scorched earth on the border
Listen to the complaints of distant sister states
Imprison some blind POWs on a bas-relief
Ward off the wind-blown sand with our shields on winter nights
    I am a bleeding soldier

Sprinkle grape wine on the date-wood guillotine
Fill the beggar's iron bowls with gold coins
Replenish the oil in the brass lamps in the temple of the gods
Light a torch on the astronomical tower to beckon the lost swan home
    I am a white-haired priest

The prince lashes my bony shoulders with a palm leaf whip
My bloody footprints fall on the long stone alley
Like an antelope I long for cool, clean water
The palanquin is just passing the fountain
    I am an obedient palanquin bearer

All weeping must be put off until tomorrow
Today we must work

Arabia

From a perfume box carved with flowers
From ragged old red turbans
From a camel's two humps
From the long, dark scabbard of a Damascus sword
From the melancholy shadow of my beard
Someone's there! Night has come
From the melancholy shadow of my beard

Many deaths lurk in a small faraway town
Or roses are trampled into the mud of a squalid alley
Or stray arrows extinguish the small flames of the holy lamps
Or a square dance
Or the whimpering of a lute
Or arabesques of smoke from a hookah
Or filthy baskets on the backs of beggars
Or Death
Ah, Ah, someone's there!
So much death

Where are the water plants?
Where are the cool, juicy coconuts?
Where is Orion?
(The desert takes a fatalistic view of my high deerskin boots)
And many gold coins have been lost again
Again, so sad
Ah, ah, someone's there!
Again, so sad

Some philosophy
Some chaotic dreams
And night has come
The axes of time chop rings of time on the forehead
The sound of a coffin being nailed shut
Ah, Ah, someone's there!
The sound of a coffin being nailed shut

Jerusalem

A small-cross-shaped star, in the South
Esau rides a donkey to the fields
To weep for one starry night
To contemplate one starry night
A small cross-shaped star, in the South

Doves bear olive branches in their bills, in the South
St. Simon bears a weighty cross
To go and wash those nail-scarred hands
To mend that holy robe
Doves bear olive branches in their bills, in the South

Seven white-clad virgins, in the South
Mary takes them to adorn that road
To spread laurels
To spread pity
Seven white-clad virgins, in the South

All the fruit has ripened, in the South
John has finished baptizing
To weave that crown of thorns
To weld that crown of iron
All the fruit has ripened, in the South

Jesus dwells in every blade of grass, in the South
A sinner shed a single day of holy life
To drown out that lake of fiery brimstone
To consume that snake of snakes
Jesus dwells in every blade of grass, in the South

Greece

Ah, Greece walks toward me
A golden cockerel sips dew at the palace
Homer strums a lyre with no strings

Ah, a lyre with no strings
I sense the fragrant warmth
Like the Aegean Sea where Helen bathed

Ah, the Aegean Sea
Venus stands on a shell
As flowers flutter down

Ah, flowers
Whose song does my heart hold?
Whose heart holds my song?

Ah, song
Moss scores the city battlements
Greece walks toward me

Rome

Spring is so lonely this year
There's a little more moss on the broken columns
This is the modern age

Virgil's poems cast many a shadow
Like streaks of tears
Bitter cypresses also cast many a shadow

Someone strolls to the Tiber
Picks a bunch of dandelions, covers his eyes
And cries all afternoon long
The Tiber cries all afternoon long too

Never is a Roman woman seen
The swallows carry nothing in their bills
Only sheep are grazing, chewing grass
Shaking the bells at their necks, shaking
      the bells at their necks

Chewing grass, shaking the bells at their necks
Shaking the bells at their necks, chewing grass

A far-traveled visitor dismounts
Saying he saw a jujube tree
Bearing small, puckery jujubes
Growing from the blind eyes of a ruined statue
Bearing small, puckery jujubes

A golden cricket sings behind a broken shield
Sings for no reason
An insectivorous rodent sniffs
    Between the toes of an ancient princess
Sniffs for no reason

The sheep are chewing grass, chewing grass
Virgil casts many shadows, many shadows
The Tiber cries all afternoon long, all afternoon

This is the modern age
There is a little more moss on the broken columns
Spring is so lonely this year

Paris

Nathaniel, what should I tell you about beds?
—Andre Gide

The soft slippers of your lips
Trampled my eyes. At dusk, at six o'clock
When a falling star knocks me senseless, Paris enters
An obscene epoch of beds

Between the evening papers and the starry sky
Someone lies in the grass bleeding
Between the roof and the dew
Rosemary blooms in the womb

You are a valley
You are a fine looking mountain blossom
You are a pie, trembling in sickly rat-gray
Rustling timidly as you eat on the sly

How much truth can a blade of grass bear? God
When eyes are accustomed to midnight's poppy
And the silky sky beneath the shoes;
   When your dodder-like veins
Wind their way south from your knees

Does last year's snow remember those coarse footprints? God
When a baby curses its umbilical cord with a tiny cry
When he covers his face passing Notre Dame next year
On his way to that obscene epoch of beds
   that holds nothing for him

You are a river
You are a blade of grass
You are last year's snow with no memory of footprints
You are sweet-scented, sweet-scented shoes

Between the Seine and reason
Who seeks death?
Between despair and Paris
The only thing holding up the sky is the Eiffel Tower

London

Ah, Virginia
At night, behind Westminster Cathedral
As the pigeons peck at the cracked bell
I am startled by your gentle cruelty
Right now on Trafalgar Square
A gas lamp endures the night
A beggar under the eaves, the stars high and far away
Daisies in the window, a sword in the past

My Virginia is in bed
Chewing on a man's beard
As a bracelet breaks and falls, a cedar groans
A small earthquake rumbles in the mattress

Your hair forms a frightening tributary
In the African Congo
Your arms possess the firmness of a magnetic field
Your eyes are like rotten leaves, your blood naked

And as a barefoot Jesus passes through the pea-soup fog
To pawn his only bloody robe
I can seize hold of nothing
Save your tea-colored breasts

It's night, at the mouth of the Thames
The briar flower between your lips
    complains about the way it was timidly plucked
A beggar under the eaves, the stars high and far away
Daisies in the window, a sword in the past

Ah Virginia, we will die before six
As all of London hides under wigs
Waiting for a black slave to serve dinner
We can harvest wheat by sowing just a penny

Chicago

City of big shoulders
They tell me you are wicked
                    —Carl Sandburg

In Chicago, we make love by pushing buttons,
    ride mechanical birds on spring outings
Pick daisies from billboards, spread a dreary culture
Under the railroad trestles

 Walking south from Seventh Street
I know your hair holds an equation
A taxi captures God's starlight
Arms spread, inhale the fragrance of mathematics

When the beauty of autumn has been electrolyzed
And your debauchery congeals with kerosene
My heart is reduced to an elegy
In a blast furnace

Sometimes the timid angels
Patrol at dusk
Their tender hands lacerated
On the electric wires between smokestacks

Still, beyond a Chinese hibiscus
Alone I whistle tying my necktie
While thinking of my old home
There's probably a fox standing on the grassy slope

That night you were mine
Like a butterfly confused in the soot
Yes, in Chicago
The only things not made of steel are the butterflies

And as the steam whistle blows with a heartless tone
Under the man-made pines in the park
Whose velvet shawl
Saved this rough, illiterate city

In Chicago, we write poems by pushing buttons,
   ride mechanical birds to view the clouds
Reap oats from billboards, yet a laughable culture
Must be built under the railroad trestles

Naples

—as seen in 1942

Why do the women made of plaster in this city
Though mutilated by steel
Always love
To smile that way
    Even as their foreheads
    Sink among briars and rubble

And when the ivy loses its last defense
Outside the long, long gallery
From the tops of burning trees
    Struck by incendiary bombs
        The angels scream
Taking flight

The foreign soldiers change the color of street slang
Chameleon-like
Sometimes the whole of Italy
Squabbles over a can of peas
In San Nicola Market in the morning

Children, many of whom
Have no name
Play on the bombed streets
Like wild pear trees
Sprouting beneath the Virgin's throne
Putting forth shoots and bitter-looking flowers
    But for whom were they planted?

Their small hands cannot grasp
The events of last summer

Nor the events of this summer
In an age when reinforced concrete is more important
    than evening prayers
Through the gray of gun covers
    God will see
The possible fathers of these kids are crestfallen
    (At the sudden loss of dignity their nation ought to have)

The next day
They are sent out to destroy
Those who wear silk shirts
    Who call black servants by tapping
        The rims of their glasses with silver spoons
Whose lives are made pale by snuff

God will witness them
Mark a cross
Across their own shadows with a bayonet, drawing out
A future for Naples
Bleaker than a poison rose

Florence

All afternoon spent
Sitting
Under the checkered umbrella of a pasta place
The China Sea dressed in a gown of light
Waits for me to the right of my boot sole

And like yesterday
After I boarded a carriage I asked myself:
Where do you want to go?
    In a wind of blue satin
    Even sadness is borrowed

And there should be something
    Hidden between poverty and the prolonged lives of daisies
At the Uffizi
    Raphael dies every minute!

And finally, after crossing the bridge
Chewing a blade of grass pulled from the riverbank
    I try hard to recall her face
    And the way she ate egg rolls that year

Spain

Flora, come to the window! Flora
In the oak grove
In the oak grove where a cat hangs
I have buried my venomous book

A rose thorn is stuck in the edge of the moon
A golden needle is clenched in the mouth of a dead man
A matador in a red scarf
A fan stirs up a scandal

Ah, it's still Madrid, Flora
Beneath the kites
Shaking under a heavy guitar
Seven small knives chase the rhythm
The bull's horns make of every moment a lifetime

No one wants to return to yesterday
The mirror plagiarizes
The velvety life in your eyes
Behind the aloeswood
My name is Frederico

Far off, among the pink fringe flowers, Flora
A toad eats your forehead
On the other side of the open balcony, Flora
A star crosses the flowing river

India

Oh Mahatma!
Wrap newborn babies in your *kasaya*
Your bosom, their warm, scented cradle
So that their tiny hands might touch your lofty brow
And your solemn whiskers fine as grass
And as they cry, let them cry out Mahatma!

Lead them to throw off womb-like blackness, Mahatma!
Raise heads of wet hair to the clear sky above the Himalayas
And see the sun, like a will-o'-the-wisp in the brain of the universe
Rise from the cold, deep Bay of Bengal
And see the bluebirds in the temples
And see chickens at the edges of wells where young girls go to draw water
Let them trace Mahatma with their tiny hands in their infancy

Mahatma, let them grow up like small white birches
Place many springs behind their eyelashes
Give them primroses, that they might smell the strong fragrance of the soil
Persimmons fall from the persimmon trees
Apples fall from the apple trees
Like blessings falling in droves from your heart
Let them find the Mahatma in the Vedas

Mahatma! Days of silence have come
Let them go to the plains, give them a hunger for the sacred
Let them go into dark chambers, give them spinning wheels
    with which to make their own clothes
Mount an elephant, play a shepherd's flute, play your brilliant past

Go to the granary, sleep on wheat and feel the fragrance of the harvest
Go to the Ganges and call the wind to fill the butterfly-like sails
Mahatma, the days of silence are yours
Let them go far away, leaving India, you, and days of silence behind

Summer has come, Mahatma
The shadow of your robe plays beneath the Bodhi tree
The Indian sun is your giant incense burner
The grassy fields of India, your giant prayer mat
Your heart is filled with Brahman and filled with nirvana
There are many songs and many sounds
Let them write Mahatma in the *Ramayana*

Sap flows abundantly in the willows and the fruit has ripened
Let them feel love, that small pain
Ah Mahatma, veil brides with the blossoms of your songs
Hiding a couple green apricots in hair filled with honeysuckle
Reciting scripture, performing rituals around the wildfire
When night comes, smear betel juice on their lips
Redden their footprints with rose balsam juice
Wash their flower-like bodies in snow-white milk
Mahatma, may you accompany the bride in her palanquin

Ah Mahatma, you too must come when they are old
When the cobra coils itself in the shadow of their gravestones
Weep for that shattered magic flute
All the white peacocks died young
The Ganges will flash bronze-colored tears
They will resemble the flowers of this spring
    the songbirds singing this summer
Transforming harsh winter into a frightful serenity
And in death think of the Mahatma

Profiles

—BOOK 5

Professor C

His stiff, white collar will support his classicism until June
Each morning he knots his tie in the prewar style
Then he takes up his walking stick and snuffbox and sets off
As he crosses the campus, that early ambition of
Becoming a statue still burgeons

And eating spinach is of no use
It was proved long ago that nothing exists beyond the clouds
When darkness bends down seeking a lantern
He says he has a huge face
Composed of countless stars at night

The Sailor

He tightens the cables dripping with salt
He climbs the high mast
At night, he lays his thought-filled head
Upon a moonlit place on deck

And the earth is round

His girl writes to him from a brothel far away
Her nickname is tattooed on his arm with a chrysanthemum
As a drizzling rain shakes the poplar behind the lighthouse
A song about him is sung in the neighborhood

And the earth is round
Oh Sea! All of this is foolishness to you

The Colonel

That is simply a different kind of rose
Born out of the flames
They fought their greatest battle in a field of buckwheat
And he lost one of his legs in '43

He has heard history and the sound of laughter

What is immortality?
Cough syrup, razor blades, and last month's rent . . .
And in the small skirmishes of his wife's sewing machine
He feels the only thing that can take him prisoner
Is the sun

The Nun

And she always feels something far off calling her
After saying a rosary
On this mackerel-colored afternoon
She still feels it

And the sea lies beyond where the ferries moor
She sits this afternoon
The bugle call from the army barracks is always the same
She sits

Tonight the wind may blow, a mandolin plays beyond the wall
Its lonely plaint passing on its way—
So it was once recorded in a book
But whatever became of the protagonist?

Secretly she wonders and thus is distracted . . .
She closes her eyes and leans on the night for a minute
Then in passing removes a carnation from the piano top
Because it pains her heart

Opera Actress

At sixteen her name was bruited about town
A sad melody

Those almond-colored arms ought to have been guarded by eunuchs
Her small coiffure broke the hearts of many a man in the Qing

It's "Jade Hall Spring"
(Every night the theatre was filled with faces
    cracking melon seeds!)
"Woe, woe is me . . ."
She sang, her arms locked in a cangue

Someone said
She had fooled around with a White Russian officer in Kiamusze

A sad melody
Cursed by women in every town

The Late Governor of a Province

When the bells tolled seven times
   his brow and loftiness came crashing down
On the night borrowed from the doctor
Under his wealth and honor but tragic skin . . .

The chorus ends

The Circus Clown

I don this red bowtie
Under black honeysuckle blossoms
Ah, Zebra, my little sweet
Under a funny fig tree
My childhood
Lies on that side of the globe and time piece

Where are we going tomorrow?
Under the unbearable striped canvas
I don this red bowtie
My fermented nose
My second face
Where are we going tomorrow?

Under purely tragic straw hats
The ladies laugh
Fluttering pagodas on their folding fans
The ladies laugh
Laugh at me mixing it up
Between a giraffe and an antelope

And she swings on the trapeze
Under ropes groaning from appendicitis
And sees me as a gloomy nail
She kisses the tightrope walker
She descends
She refuses any trace of my spring

Under black honeysuckle blossoms
Ah, Leopard, my little sweet
The moonlight shines through your iron bars
Throwing a checkered flannel robe over you
Under a funny fig tree
I don this red bowtie

The Forsaken Woman

A woman wounded by flowers
Spring isn't her real enemy

Never again will her skirt
Form a pretty, dizzying circle
Nor will the night of her black hair
Ever cause that young man without a lantern
    to lose his way
The river of her age flows backwards
She is no longer the maid of this spring

The lute taken up by that man
Breaks and falls into doleful silence
The thief of love has fled
The magnetic fields of men no longer point north

She is no longer
The maid of this spring
She hates to hear the sound of her blood
Dripping on the name of that man
She hates praying even more
Because Jesus was also a man

The Mad Woman

—pitiful Beiwei sits in the road
and again begins to chew her shoes

If you laugh again I'll lift the street
Lift it beyond the control of the police,
   to the chaotic starry sky
Where the police whistle doesn't reach
Laugh, laugh, laugh again, laugh again
Mary will make a noose of the rainbow and hang you all

I sit before the furious image of Moses
All the turbulent rivers of Africa are hidden in my hair
I sit. I let the sirocco blow over me
Let the noise of the city polish my breasts
I sit. Mary adopts me
I'll follow after her. I am a proper girl

I wrinkle my brow for antiquity
Proper wrinkles
I'm not this present name
Father died in the battle of Athens
   Leaving behind a gray-haired girl
Yes, laugh, you ought to laugh. That girl is me
I'm not this present name

Who told you to tear off that lavender blouse and divide
Your naked body among the boys, whom you love and don't love
Boys in skin-tight flannel trousers

Boys who play tennis, boys kissed and forgotten
Heartless boys. But Mary, you have no idea how I agonized
Over which one I should give my soul

Mary, why do you insist that I keep on being Beiwei?
Why must I be this Beiwei?
Beiwei! Which of her outfits displease him?
The tablecloth is white with red checks
The water in the goldfish bowl has been changed
Mary, pluck out Beiwei's brown pupils
And compare them to those of that cheap floozy

At seven in the morning, just like you
I can see the sun setting
And I love your eyes and the way they surround me
Encircling me in a small wall of eyes
A shining house of eyes, the eye's house
So I say: sleep, Mary, sleep

One eye gives me a flower
One eye gives me a candle
One eye gives me a bed of moss
One eye tickles me, but I don't laugh
I know who I am, I am . . .
I'm a bird, or
Or, it just so happens, I'm a pair of shoes

Khrushchev

Khrushchev is a man
Who climbed out of a chimney
In Russia, his name sets forests atremble
He often rides on a broom
Scaring women and children
He often crosses Gorky Park
To wash his bloody hands in a fountain

But all the old men
Know Khrushchev is a good man
Even though he pinched out all the candles in the churches
Even though he greases his whip with baby fat
Even though he brushes his teeth with the ribs of the poor
He really is a good man

Yes, Khrushchev is a good man
His shirts are washed cleaner than
The snows of Petersburg by slaves
He swigs vodka
He's full of wisecracks
At night he bolts the iron doors of the Kremlin
Because he can't stand to hear the sobbing outside
He is so compassionate
He's a good man

Yes, Khrushchev is a good man
He's got a bad earache
So he needs the secret police
He loves to control people with barbed wire

He loves to bathe the country in fresh blood
He does not concern himself with the people
Just their obedience

Yes, Khrushchev is a good man
He strangles Czechoslovakia
So that it might breathe
He shakes hands with Poland with a bayonet
And uses tanks
To plow Hungary
He really is a good man

Nobody throws him out of Moscow
Nobody throws him out of cold Red Square
So the people of Georgia go on gnawing black bread
So the people of the Caucasus go on wearing shackles
So the people of the Ukraine go on shedding blood
All because they have
A man as good as Khrushchev

Weeds
—BOOK 6

For My Wife

I always like the way you
Sit, hair hanging loose, playing a little Debussy
On a slip of burdock leaf
On clouds in the river
The blue sky, a Han dynasty blue
The ancient tenderness of Christ
Amid the chirping of sparrows at the far-off watermill
When the month of May is near

(Let them shout long live creeping wood sorrel)

Oh, one whole life is such a long, long time
Even though a curse stops for good
Where the clarinet and contralto vertical bamboo flutes are
How beautiful to think about him from morning to night,
        thinking how beautiful he is

Thinking, living, occasionally smiling
Neither happy nor unhappy
Something flutters above your head
Perhaps
Nothing ever has

Beautiful sheaths of grain are often deployed on the fields
He always kisses where he likes to kiss
Did you ever see the rain falling on the tree leaves and grass?
To be blades of grass and leaves
Or a rain shower
According to your wishes

(Let them shout long live their creeping wood sorrel)

You love to recite "Slow Slow Song" in the afternoon
Manicure your nails and sit drinking tea
Ah, a whole life is a long long, time
On the forehead of the past
Through words grown weary
Ah a whole life is a long, long time
Buffeted by song
And regret

No one is allowed to talk that way
That kind of talk, that kind
Confused and lost
Far away, far, far away

For R. G.

By the waterside are many thick-lipped women.
They quarrel using all possible allotted
Colors. And autumn days push away from the
   face of the clock to seek a different glory,
 In their gloomy hair.

This aimless smile rises continuously to stop the stars.

Melons are displayed
On the other side of form.
This is an unbearable tangle of afternoon light.
One foot set on wild fennel, the other
Scuttles off and falls in the river.

Eyes are planted between four walls,
A kind of sparkling field.
And the remaining half of the song
Is still kept in the mouth where the clarinet
Leans.

Pale flesh is initially compelled to obey,
In the rectangle of night
Belonging solely to the window.

That handsome fellow. Handsome R. G.

Fine days and unscrupulous friends
And death not contained in parentheses
That handsome fellow R. G.

In Memory of T. H.

When they arrived it was nearly over
So they washed his body
Dressed him in new clothes
Relieved him of certain chemical exertions
   The moonlight shines
      The river flows—
      On the windowsill some medicine bottles and furniture
         A car goes by   someone shouts, selling lilies of the valley
         But no angels

They pick him up and carry him outside
They cross a bridge and put him in an alley
A woman comes and cries, another begins to shake him
The yellow of the Algerian desert, the green of the Adriatic Sea
The magnificent landscape around Milan
Apricot trees in spring and all of next year's plagues
   And it's already too late

   In a pile of yellowing medical history cards
   In a cry softer than silk
   Back to the world
   A face
   Falls speeding

Burning Incense as an Offering for T. H.

Poets, I don't know how you
Found them
Among layer upon layer of the dead and
The dead
What part of nature did your calcium carbonate visage join?
Stars and night
Birds or men
On the leaves
In the rain
On a distant whaling ship
In the deeply sunken quilt of hospital room 104
When the first rays of the morning sun were withdrawing?

Every night behind the old house on the hill
   a cricket sings its endless song
Spring advances through the tree limbs
Taking on another form
From the depths of all looks
White camellias in full bloom
Both near and far
Their fingertips greet you
They breathe
The pleasant night you left
The lamplight
And those parting words

And it's all over
The wonderful days, begun in blackness
Women jump over
The weakening pulse of
Your plant's underground stem

See how the low sky
Over an area of clay
Behind a pottery figurine and water pitcher
Is suddenly deprived of
All beauty

As for poetry, that foolish thing, you have seen its substance;
On our poor supper table
The bones we sucked and scraped clean
—That most exquisite sentence?
When your mouth opens for the unknown
Your poems
With all manner of praise
Desert you and live on their own
And your hands
Tremble deeply for their later years

For a Surrealist

—for the days spent with Shang Qin

Your yesterday weds your tomorrow
You have a child not named Today
Your song is a jacket draped over dogs
Fish fly in the sky
Birds swim in the water
Your kneecaps don't recognize
Your own toes
You are last winter's
Final heresy
As well as the very first heresy
Of spring this year

You sing: sweet pear tree, sweet pear tree
At five in the morning
In a number of filthy alleys
You place a Bible under the pillow of a prostitute
The story of Moses and Mt. Sinai is forgotten
At five in the morning
Sweet pear tree, sweet pear tree, you sing

You long to smell the buckwheat fragrance of another world
To break everything to smithereens
And put it all back together again
To unite past and present, weaving Helen

and the peddling girl at the train station
Mountains and seas, a wandering monk gathering pine cones and a black sailor
Conceptualization and non-conceptualization, a windy and windless sky
You are a child sobbing terribly
A one-eyed child who unknowingly
Places love on his forehead

Nightmares will burn you to death in the end
Like a skyscraper
Sandburg's iron spike
Destroyed by lightning
But you have nothing to do with Sandburg
He holds the people tightly in his grasp
Whitman's popularity has passed and the old songs now seem out of date
You have nothing to do with logic
The spike of logic
Nor anything to do with poetry

What are you?
  (Sweet pear tree, sweet pear tree)
Where are you from?
  (At five in the morning, numerous cold stars)
Where are you going?
  (numerous cold stars, at five in the morning)

And you too are an existence
Like maple sugar
Stirred into the developer
For no reason
But it is an existence
That resembles the water hyacinth
Under a black and gold shroud

Lips

—in memory of Y. H.

Thick
Lips
That never told lies
Lips
That told fairy tales
Lips
That denied a kiss by a lovely girl
    Lips as sad as a rose
        Oh such sad lips

We will kiss you
And though there are
Many of us
Who do not know you
We will kiss you
Your lonely, particular
    Lips as sad as a rose
        Oh such sad lips

And we also give you
A small flower
A little wine
And all of spring
And
We will bring a passel of poor country kids
To fly kites for you
And

Have each of them in turn
With their lips, after eating millet
Kiss your cold killed
    Lips as sad as a rose
        Oh such sad lips

Thinking of a Friend

. . . afterwards we cried
When the setting sun and the mallows
Broke, falling together over
The ancient dwellings in the North

The sound of the fortune-telling gong
Drifts blindly into the distance
I imagine it must at this very moment
    be passing through the carved archway
Honoring a chaste woman
    Dong! Dong!
Answering a woodpecker
Then falling silent again

In the dim study
Your scarcely visible bust
Forever listens to
The bookworms tell of hatreds in the book collection
Forever stares
At the shadows of pine trees
    stitched on the paper windows
Like the tear stains on Grandma's old silk blouse

    Dong, dong
The sound of the fortune-telling gong fades
Into the distance
Singing the tale of those long alleys
Of the eyes of the lion door knocker
Weeping blood

I remember I was ill then
Sitting weakly in an old rattan chair
Writing verse in memory of my departed mother

The boy servant rode a mule
To deliver the poems to my departed mother
Amid the rustling leaves
Tongues of flame read them for her

And often on the chilly windowsill
I find mallow flowers from some unknown sender
As well as freshly picked jujubes
Secretly
Placed on the garden swing

Till one night I discovered someone
Under the sycamore tree
Carving my name
And her name with a small knife
Inside the same heart
          it turned out she was the girl I'd met
Last summer washing her feet by the river
. . . later we wept together

Setting Out from Sensations
—BOOK 7

Setting Out

We've set sail. Under a mortal or immortal
Sun of brass,
In a wind devoid of angels,
The sea is only blue for itself.

The mast's shadow
Is clenched between the teeth.
From the stern we watch our seventeenth year swirling in the wake.
And on deck we finish pacing the length of a sigh, on the smile she
Laid for me as a blanket in the past
I sit, thinking in silence all afternoon.

Tonight there will be an assassination in Havana! A threat
Seeks an address. Gray bats circle the rear portico of city hall
With a sad beauty, a piano opens its black umbrella.

  (How pitiful! Her sleep
  between chrysanthemums and hawthorns.)

They have days crowded with
  More faces
  More postmen
  More streets
  More despair, despair, despair than during the grandest market.
On that enormous ship that finally sinks into the mud
They clamor with the voice of irrational eyes
They cling to their own ramie-like nervous systems
  forgetting the scissors . . .

Appropriately
They suffer this tragedy.
This makes me overjoyed
I stand to port, consign my tie to the wind, and smile

Andante Cantabile

The necessity of tenderness
The necessity of affirmation
The necessity of a little wine and sweet osmanthus flowers
The necessity of politely watching a girl walk by
The necessity of realizing that you are not Hemingway
The necessity of war in Europe, rain, cannons, weather, and the Red Cross
The necessity of strolling
The necessity of walking the dog
The necessity of mint tea
The necessity of rumors like grass

Swaying every evening at seven o'clock at the far end of the stock exchange
The necessity of revolving doors. The necessity of penicillin. The necessity
Of assassinations. The necessity of evening papers.
The necessity of wearing flannel trousers. The necessity of parimutuel tickets.
The necessity of inheritances from paternal aunts
The necessity of balconies, oceans, and smiles
The necessity of being languid

But once being considered a river, it must continue to flow
That's the way the world has always been:—
Guan Yin on a distant mountaintop
Poppies in poppy fields

Afternoon

It's hard to say if we won't result in brilliance
Dipper gourds and dogwoods insist
On last year's tunes
There's no need to search any further
Sappho works in the bakery across the street
    And so it goes, and before long it's afternoon
Unable to be brilliant, we smile and worry
A few of yesterday's
Unfinished deaths
Die under the electric power poles

(Behind the blinds, I think of you, I think of you
    on the city's blue cobblestone streets)

Indifferent to an even bigger joke
Ulysses is seen begging by the railroad tracks
Offer up to God any danger of your choice
If you chance to wake up on the wrong night
To discover Truth
Is on that side of a wound
If a whole cannon disappears beneath the sands

(I think of you amidst the ballads between grays and reds of silks,
      agates, and tuberoses)

The boy in the red jacket has a handsome face
He shoots baskets alone on the court
Pigeons build nests at the back of city hall
The river flows of its own accord

And so it goes, and before long it's afternoon
Nothing's happened, that's for sure
Each head forgets something different

(Gently recall beautiful Xianyang City)

Forty-five minutes past midnight, a drowned man's clothes
    Drift ashore
And embracing her in bed surpasses
The excavation of Greece
After the sound of an electric trolley fades
The Epicureans begin to sing

—Can the teeth in the grave answer these?
Monday, Tuesday, Wednesday, all the days?
Spontaneous Nocturne

His watch stopped at four o'clock
The world was under his hair
The pillow looked pallid
He'd just come back from a duel
Recorded on vellum
On a small street dead for a thousand years
A young man forgot his sword and his name
A dissipating beauty
A Phoenician on a pottery dish
A Dodge drives by, a star
    inclines toward a billboard ad for shampoo
        another has been there for ages

The night is between a black man's forehead and chocolate
Daybreak has not yet come

Umbrellas are abandoned everywhere
Moonlight ages, the market is fast asleep
A house is sad at heart for being a house
Much waiting is waiting
Gazing endlessly
At the arriving road
A dead man's glass eye

The lamplight will always be handed down
Christ's horse lies in a crypt
You are in your own city
After a bout of coughing comes the so-called second coming
The owner of the photo studio opens the door
The tree leaves glisten
The sound of the propeller
On a low-flying aircraft

Nocturne

No matter what, the coming days must be scattered for the rats.
Friday. The top of a skull has been nailed to a charred wall,
The female servant's complaints of last night
Bacteria-like, depressingly
Sprout over a discarded dinner plate
And in Africa, many poisonous roses take flight with a shout
And the pupils of my eyes are anxious to cast me aside
To join the crane and its cold iron-colored cries.

(The bell tolled seven times and thought once of Jesus)

The city arrived on a ladder of moonlight
Reaching the top of a cactus.
The flags could help laughing
Each window ruminates on its own inlaid face
And a boot nail has no idea who stomped it into my brains.
The steam whistle blows for a moment
    The workers are off
        That woman goes home, up the escalator . . .
Her false teeth and desires firmly grasped in hand.

As the electric guitar begins to tell a lie.
We end up sitting on a sofa,
Dragging the corpse
Out of the river of the evening paper
With our own eyes

So It Is When Night Falls

Some girls are out in the hallway, some girls are in the room
Some can never let go of that song, some dance three steps
Some joke, some recline there, some feign sadness
The bird and its nest, war and its peace
Life is one thing, Truth another

(How I learned to stop worrying and love the bomb)

Some kiss Colonel K, some eat peaches
Some have never heard anything about her daddy
Some say better start right away, some say it's already too late
Heaven is beaver's wood, Thursday is honey
The soul is a phone number, but a lover is a pearl

(How I learned to stop worrying and love the bomb)

So when night falls
Its beginning is signaled by a bugle
Neon lights cough violently
The city noises leap into the mirror
A river without banks, a slot machine gnaws
Penicillin and other drugs
Amid screams, trembling, and on powdered faces
    However brilliant you may want her to be
       Is how much brilliance she gives you

And writing poems and playing poker and losing one's temper
    Are not problems
Dreams are one thing, bombs another
So it is when night falls

The Courtyard

Nobody can rescue him from behind the power plant
From his wife, from the wind, from the after-dinner nagging
From the courtyard filled with autumn bristle grass

Nobody can save him from after work
From his sister's letter, from a velvet shawl, from cold cream
From the complete distortion of a face cleaned under the corridor
And from unintentionally leading troops to attack Hungary
Or an evening spent writing in a pile of red books
At the critical moment night and dawn are welded together
Or that never-thought-of, so-called "perhaps"

So go to sleep, Sea!

If she suddenly cries
If she insists that way is bad
If she brings up that early affair with his cousin
Just sleep, sleep your sleep
Full-rounded sea!

Easter

She walks south along Dehui Street
After September she no longer seems to like
The man she loved before the war
The rest is not all that clear

Or the river, the stars, or the night
Or a bouquet of flowers, a guitar, or spring
Or who should bear responsibility for an unspecified fault
Or something else

—And it's almost impossible to compose a song out of this
Even though she walks south along Dehui Street
And occasionally lifts her head
To glance at that row of toothpaste ads.

A Common Song

On that side of the caltrops is the elementary school, a little farther
        on the sawmill
Next door is Aunt Su's garden where she grows lettuce and corn
To the left of the three maple trees and some other stuff
Farther on you hit the post office, the tennis courts
    and directly to the west, the train station
At this moment clouds are floating above the drying laundry
As for sadness hiding somewhere in the vicinity of the railroad tracks
It's always this way
May has come
And quietly accepts all of this without complaint

At 5:45 the freight train passes
The river ties a gorgeous knot under the bridge and flows away
When the grasses here set off to occupy the distant graveyard
Never noticed by the dead
But most importantly
Over there on the balcony
A boy is eating a peach
May has come
It matters not under whose eaves eternity is building its nest
Quietly accepting all of this without complaint

Setting Out from Sensations

As far as I am concerned, to live is to think.
—W. H. Auden

I

These days are but an echo. I am struggling to remember . . .
Whose other eye was really left behind
On the platter of sturgeon on the breakfast table

And the umbilical cord is discarded at random, someone leaves
    his dentures in the window to dry in the sun
Their intimate words of last night are like a monstrous snake
    swallowing flowers

These days are but echoes. A black flag struggles out of a citadel
Leading jawless troops, transformed again into sick mice
Fleeing from a ravine of abysmal blackness

Ah, these days are but echoes! How frightening
He pulls his feet from my splattered brains
This is the lizard that firmly grasped a constellation, this is
Clay risen from the grave

And as the butterflies cry in a flowerless wood
Whose blood is sprinkled on the crowns of the gods?

This is a saintly one-eyed woman
Bluebonnets dare not approach her
This is a bed sheet
The love erected on the bed sheet

And when autumn's gold coinage slipped from her nipples
I believe there was a star high over France that night

Glorious days borne from the echoes
That's my name, swept aside by the mirror's cry of alarm
In the darkness of the government office
Once again seeping into history, history's dangerous shoals

2

Through a ladder of ribs
Suspended from a hawthorn, through the breath of a jujube
Tree behind the arsenal, through black, silken drumbeats

The long rosters of those forever departed
From clocks and calendars

Under the grinning corn in the moonlight
During the impassioned speech of a Mauser
In the emptiness beneath a pile of hair under camouflage netting
Between a cactus and a weary Bible

Through the faces of the dead layered one upon another
In the wind, through the whiteness
Of the surnames on the crosses

Through Colonel S's fine memory
Announcing to me why a man traced the line of battle
With a bayonet on the buckwheat
Why he shuns his soul like a toad a lily pad
When night weaves steel in the cellar

Carrying me so as not to frighten me, in the final days
Making me understand the hateful cold
The invisible silence in the dark
The deep, deep sleep, my miserable sisters

This then is me, this year's popular explanation
Merely for the silk belt of an outer garment
They sell me to Death

Between shadows
Between parting and meeting
Where my eyes are not, those times
Under the grinning corn in the moonlight

3

Like a voice carrying off a song, child,
    a ball of lead carried me away
Like a cruel woman suddenly holding back her tongue
Like a meteor shower twinkling for a moment, I had finished
Autumn at the other end of the shell's trajectory

Like night, a strange blanket
Separates our kisses from the explosions
Like removing an old flannel garment, I am cast off
The past dragging a gray shadow

And I too was a kite-flying child
A child in a swing watching the clouds
A traveling child striking brass cymbals
A crying child whose mother left him future sunsets
In her dying will

When this eye cannot answer another eye
When columbine and grass spread over your chest
When buttons prove triumphant over time, when the
Tiny echo suddenly lost its soul

As usual, the elderberry
Is thickly overgrown with moss, as usual the stalk of grass
Vainly sways the night, as usual at dawn
A pale sun rises from the hands of a poker player

Some banners flutter and fall
Fall and flutter
Some wombs empty then fill
Fill then empty

And when a giant sickle screams to take possession
Of silently rotting meat somewhere else
I recognize in every quarter of the nakedness
Your foreheads in the tangled grass

Oh Death, perhaps your name is this beauty touched with blood
Those faces piled one upon another, the jawless troops
Oh Death, perhaps your name is this beauty touched with blood
The cold cry of butterflies
This long, deep sleep, my miserable sisters

Under the low-hanging, lying sky of stars
In the false dusk knit of false prayers
In the newly lit section of town you are approaching
In those times when my eyes were not there

And my echoing heart will never rest
Running madly towards sudden downpours in May

In damp shoes brushing past a high cliff
Look! A dance-obsessed girl

As these days are but echoes borne of anxiety
Swept away amidst the mirror's cry of alarm
On a platter of sturgeon waiting to be chosen by someone
In the darkness of a government office
Trembling on a bed sheet

One dance-obsessed girl
One chronology of sensations

For H. Matisse

—The People of Montparnasse

I

Once more they will call it brilliant, Matisse
Two eyes set Notre Dame aflame, from amidst the play
The nakedness of the room slowly ascends to tickle the angels
Without an echo, a leopard crouches in the darkness
Weaving all that is strange, your hands tear and scatter your hair
And in the raucous playing of an electric guitar
At the dangerous boundary of some dream
The golden women lying
On a patchwork quilt of roses
Await you, Henri Matisse
Matisse, the glorious shame

For the accumulated rumors on a pillow, in summer
The silks are shocked but you are ignorant in the dark
And what the women want is a small wound
A velvet moment
Or feigned resistance to you
Plagiarized from the mirror
Or look at a pitcher from behind
The air on her thighs
Savage but tender

Matisse, I know it's not your intention
To transform all things into death
The pomegranate once fully consumed your time too, in Paris
A bedside look is such risky business

The unrestrained night, the giddy walls
A deafening roar! A Prussian blue sun
Ah, what wondrous days, Matisse
You've surely become the trusted follower of women's skin
Then how many faces do they really have?
But colors are so deceitful, and there are
Always some rhymes
Among the laughter and banter
Flowing into the heart of daybreak

2

Rainbow days
You explain the fragrant silence of a woman's frock
You explain the darkness inside breasts
(a flower blooms the whole night through!)
You explain a neck slowly consumed with kisses. After twelve
It's so easy for their eyes
To be hyacinths

In your burning palms, women cry for help with a big daub of red
You smile, rushing as if it were the first time
Sketching a Persian carpet in the room of someone else's wife
And except for the fat and the complaints
In the game purchased between a lifted and rocking quilt
Except lying down every night for someone, Matisse
Morning doesn't last forever
The women no longer need meaning

All of this is a passing guest
Women's entire history ends with their postures
    as they manicure their nails under a lamp
Even a river has a body made of speed

And nothing is born out of their hair
Dusk. The bells toll seven times
No one is about to die for anything. There's no news
And the way you paint them, they know nothing;
Looking at your sketch in black, they always ask:
Jasmine? Is that a jasmine flower? Ah, a jasmine flower
(Only the newspapermen answer them!)
Only you, Matisse
Sign your name on their plump feet
Give them a face
A sigh

3

Weave years from a swinging violet-colored thread
Make the rainbows emit perfume, make cloth sing
Your beautiful deterrent is a delicate sigh that lifts five dances
Women's captive eyes express the fineness of thin lotus cakes
As the bitterness of the daily routine comes like a bat
A prostitute bends over to wash and from a small lead tube
You squeeze out a sonata
And half of Paris

Wasting all the light to shout for Death
Stooping into a grave to dig up some blue
Only with regard to this unbarred spring season
Does your long silk ladder not know where to hang
The bed sheets lead south, in this tumult as sweet as honey
Moaning, they take you captive and against them you place a seal's breath
And people say it's splendid whenever blood drips
A room, a hall, a pitcher of homesickness
A Matisse who won't listen

Because of that reconstructed violet
Many are the souls who take part in your merrymaking
Mercury falls on account of that smile
Because you trick them into sleep, despite
The fact that under their heads
A huge landslide
Is pillowed from the beginning . . .

And Matisse, you are always sensible
When the pedestrians on Riviera Street resemble a bad melody
You ride your filthy palette
Toward that slowly inclining sky
Turn against the wind, and ascend

Abyss

I want to exist, nothing but to exist; at the same time
I am aware of the misery of existence.
        —Sartre

Children often lose their way in the thatch of your hair
The first spring torrent is concealed behind the desolate pupils of your eyes
A part of time calls out. The body launches the night's festivities
By the poisonous light of the moon, on a delta of blood
Souls rise up like serpents and strike at that haggard forehead
Suspended on the cross.

This is absurd—in Spain
No one will give him even a crumb from the crummiest wedding cake!
And we mourn everything. We spend all morning just to touch the hem
       of his gown.
Later his name is written on the wind, on a flag.
Later he tosses the leftovers of his life
To us.

Go look, go play at being sad, go smell the decay of time
We are too lazy ever to know ourselves.
Work, stroll, salute the crooks, smile and become immortal.
How they cling to maxims!
This is the face of day; open sores moan; skirts conceal a myriad of germs
The metropolis, Libra's scales, a paper moon, telephone pole language
(Today's official notices are pasted over yesterday's)
The cold-blooded sun shivers constantly
In the pale abyss wedged
Between two nights.

Time, cat-faced time,

Time, stuck fast to the wrist, time that sends flag signals.

On a night when rats weep, those who were murdered are murdered again.

They knot grass from graves into ties, they chew the Lord's Prayer stuck
          between their teeth

No skull can truly ascend to a place among the stars

To bathe his crown of thorns in resplendent blood

In the thirteenth month, the fifth season of the year, when Heaven
          appears below.

And we erect a monument to the moths attracted to last year's lamps.
          We live.

We cook wheat in wire mesh. We live.

Through the sad rhymes of the billboards, through the filthy shadows
          of concrete

Through the soul released from the ribcage

Hallelujah! We live. Walk, cough, argue

Shamelessly take up space on the earth.

Nothing is dying at the moment

Today's clouds plagiarize yesterday's.

In March I hear the cherries shout.

Countless wagging tongues bring about the fall of spring. And green flies
          nibble her face

Her calves flash from *qipao* slits

     which are longing for some people to read her,

To enter her to labor inside her body. Nothing is certain

Other than this and death. Existence is the wind, the noise on the
          threshing ground

Existence is the outpouring of a whole summer's desire for ladies

Who love to be tickled.

Beds are sinking everywhere in the night. A feverish light
Sounds like footfalls on broken glass. A farm implement forced
      to till blindly.
A translation of peach-colored flesh, a frightful language composed of
Kisses; the first meeting of blood and blood, a flame, a fatigue!
A vigorous shove that shunts her aside
At night, beds are sinking everywhere in Naples.

A woman sits at the end of my shadow. She weeps
As an infant is buried amid mock strawberries and saxifrage. . . .
The following day we go back to watch the clouds, laugh, and sip
      plum juice
On the dance floor, we dance away what little dignity remains.
Hallelujah! I'm still alive. My shoulders still carry my head
Carry existence and nonexistence
Carry a face that wears trousers.

No one knows who is next; perhaps the church mouse, perhaps the color
      of the sky.
We said goodbye ages ago to that long-hated umbilical cord.
Kisses hang suspended on the lips, religion is imprinted on the face,
We saunter, each with his own coffin lid on his back!
And you are the wind, a bird, the color of the sky, a river with no mouth.
You are the standing ashes of the dead, unburied Death.

No one has plucked us from the earth. Look at life with both eyes shut.
Jesus, don't you hear the dark wood murmuring in his brain?
Some are knocking under the sugar beet field, others under the myrtle . . .
When faces change color like chameleons, how can the torrent
Capture the reflections? When their eyes are glued to the
Darkest pages of history!

And you are nothing;
You aren't the type who breaks his cane over the face of the age
Or dance with the morning light tangled around their heads
In this city without shoulders, your book will be pulped for paper
        on the third day.
You wash you face with night, and duel with shadows
You consume your inheritance, the bride's trousseau, the weak shouts
        of the dead
You come out of your room and go back in again, rubbing your hands
You are nothing.

How can you strengthen the legs of a flea?
Inject music into the throat, force the blind to drink up all the rays of light!
Sow seeds in the palm of a hand, squeeze moonlight from between
        the breasts
—you are part of the nights that are stacked against you and spinning
        round you
Beautiful and alluring, the lovely women are yours.
A flower, a jug of wine, a bed of teases, and a date.

This is the abyss—between the pillows and the bedding—pale as a
        funeral couplet
These are girls with young faces, this is a window, this is a mirror, this
        is a small compact.
This is a smile, this is blood, these are silk ribbons waiting to be disentangled
That night, Mary's image on the wall vacated the frame, she had fled
In search of the River Lethe to wash the shameful things she had heard
        from her ears
But this is an old tale, like a rotating shadow lantern; senses, senses, senses
In the morning I hawk the sins in my basket on the streets
The sun jams its awns into my eyes.
Hallelujah! I'm still alive.

Work, stroll, salute the crooks, smile and become immortal.
Exist for the sake of existence, watch the clouds for the sake of
        watching them
Shamelessly take up space on earth.
A sleigh stops on the banks of the Congo
No one knows how it managed to slide so far
A sleigh no one knows stops there.

Afterword

Ya Hsien 瘂弦 (Ya Xian) is the penname of Wang Ching-Lin 王慶麟 (Wang Qinglin). Born in Nanyang County, Henan Province, he was active in Taiwan's Modernist Movement in the 1950s and 1960s. He is best known for a single collection of poetry titled *Abyss* 深淵, published in 1968, and an expanded edition in 1971. He stopped writing poetry altogether in the mid-1960s. The remarkable brevity of his career as a poet, from about 1953 to 1965, belies the longstanding influence his work has had in Taiwan. His poetry combines elements of traditional poetics and folksong with the various schools of modern poetry including Surrealism.

As a youngster, Ya Hsien received a modest education, but was always fond of literature, including world literature in translation. In 1949, at the age of seventeen, he joined the army and followed the Nationalists to Taiwan at the end of the civil war with the Communists. In college, he studied drama, and eventually taught the subject. After graduating from a Nationalist cadre school, he was assigned to the Navy and, in 1953, while stationed at Zuoying in southern Taiwan, he met Lo Fu and Chang Mo, two other naval officers interested in poetry. The three of them founded the Epoch Poetry Society, the oldest poetry society still active today in Taiwan.

Ya Hsien took an active role in editing the *Epoch Poetry Quarterly*. In 1959 his *Poems from Ya Hsien* 瘂弦詩抄 was published in Hong Kong. His second collection, *Abyss* 深淵 appeared in 1968 and in an expanded edition in 1971. In 1977 his *Personal Anthology* 瘂弦自選集 included all of the poems in *Abyss*, as well as early uncollected poems. In 1981 *Collected Poems of Ya Hsien* 瘂弦詩集 appeared; it reprints his *Personal Anthology*.

Ya Hsien is also a student of literary history. In 1981 his *Studies in Modern Chinese Poetry* 中國新詩研究 collected the essays he had written for the *Epoch Poetry Quarterly* on various poets from the pre-1949 era, as well as two other essays written specifically for the collection.

In the years since Ya Hsien stopped writing poetry he has continued to be active in literary circles as a lecturer, researcher, and editor. In 1968 he attended the Writer's Workshop at the University of Iowa. Then he attended the University of Wisconsin, Madison, from which he received an MA in East Asian Studies. After retiring in 1971 with the rank of Lieutenant Commander, he taught and edited a series of magazines, eventually editing the influential literary supplement of the *United Daily News*. He now calls Vancouver home, but spends a good deal of time in Taiwan and China.

★ ★ ★

Ya Hsien's best known collection is *Abyss*. It is a key work of the second wave of Chinese modernism and consists of sixty poems that are divided into seven sections, each showing a slightly different character in terms of style or theme. The first section titled "Wild Water Chestnuts" consists of twelve poems, many dealing with contemporary themes such as ennui or melancholy, but written in a folksong mode, comparable in tone to Garcia-Lorca's *Gypsy Ballads*. Ya Hsien acknowledges that Rilke was an early influence and cites his poem "Spring Days" 春日 as an example.

The second section is titled "Wartime"; some poems such as "Red Corn" 紅玉米 continue in the folksong mode, while others such as "Salt" 鹽 is a prose poem written in the modernist style. The third section titled "Songs without Music" includes seven poems on seafaring themes.

The fourth section titled "Collection of Broken Columns" contains thirteen poems all about various countries or capitals and major cities of the world. The poet tells us that he has never been to any of these places, and his treatment is imaginative. In these poems, he tends to focus on a theme and images that he associates with the locations. The section includes a number of fine and memorable poems including "Chicago" 芝加哥 and "On the Streets of China" 在中國街上, both of which satirize modern life. As might be expected, the satire in "Chicago" focuses on modern technology, while "On the Streets of China" juxtaposes

138

traditional Chinese culture and modernity, replete with the poet's humorous refrain "And poets wear corduroy suits".

The fifth section "Profiles" includes ten poems that are all portraits of various types of characters, with one poem titled "Khrushchev." The finest poem in the section is probably "The Colonel" 上校, an understated and sympathetic portrait of an army officer who has survived a war but lost a limb; a former war hero, he lives out the remainder of his life in poverty and alienation. "Professor C" C 教授 is a wonderful poem satirizing the vanities of modern life.

The sixth section "Useless Weeds" includes seven poems dedicated to the poet's wife and friends. The seventh and final section "Starting Out from Sensations" contains twelve poems, many of which are quite long and ambitious. Two of the most important poems are "For H. Matisse" 獻給馬蒂斯 and "Abyss" 深淵. As bright and colorful as a Matisse painting, the poem is less about the French painter than it is about life and art. The title poem of the collection shows the influence of T.S. Eliot and seeks to capture, in critical fashion, the sense of modern existential angst and alienation reminiscent of *The Wasteland*. A particularly complex poem, it contains the original imagery and modernist poetics we have come to expect from the poet. Although considered a signature work, it is perhaps less immediately appealing than many of his shorter lyrical poems.

The sheer variety and virtuosity exhibited by the collection have made *Abyss* a modern classic. Ya Hsien's art is one of synthesis; he is able to weave together disparate threads of tradition and the modern to create something unique. His poetry runs the gamut from realism to surrealism, incorporating elements of folksong and modernist poetics, to create poems with a wide emotional range, while also deftly capturing the critical spirit of the times. This collection is a seminal work that has had profound influence on generations of contemporary poets from Taiwan and China.

—*John Balcom*

Acknowledgments

This translation has evolved over the years and I would like to thank a number of individuals and organizations for the support and assistance they have provided. First of all, I wish to express my gratitude to Ya Hsien for his undivided support. Special acknowledgement is due to Mr. Tung Hsien-tzu for funding this translation and for his ongoing efforts to promote literature from Taiwan abroad. A number of people have read and commented on the translations over the years, for which I am grateful: Nancy Ing, Chi Pang-yuan, William Matheson, Robert Hegel, Joseph Allen, and, of course, my wife Yingtsih. I would also like to thank Christopher Mattison of Zephyr Press for his continuing editorial support. Some of these translations originally appeared in *The Taipei Chinese PEN*, and I would like to thank them for permission to reprint them with minor changes. Lastly, I would like to dedicate this translation to the memory of my beloved father Dr. Francis H. Balcom.

JOHN BALCOM holds a PhD in Chinese and Comparative Literature from Washington University in St Louis. An award winning translator of Chinese literature, philosophy, and children's books, he teaches translation at the Middlebury Institute of International Studies at Monterey, where he directed the Chinese program for many years. His translations include *Taiwan's Indigenous Writers: An Anthology of Stories, Essays, and Poems*, *After Many Autumns: An Anthology of Chinese Buddhist Literature*, *There's Nothing I Can Do When I Think of You Late at Night* by Cao Naiqian, and *Trees without Wind* by Li Rui. He is a past president of the American Literary Translators Association.

Also Available from Zephyr Press by John Balcom:

ISBN 978-0-939010-83-7   Lo Fu *Driftwood*
ISBN 978-0-981552-11-8   Lo Fu *Stone Cell*
ISBN 978-0-938890-07-9   Xiang Yang *Grass Roots*